Seasons
of a
Woman's Life

Carol Goodman Heizer, M.Ed.

Seasons of a *Woman's Life*

Carol Goodman Heizer, M.Ed.

*A*lpha Publishing
a division of
Alpha Consulting
Louisville, Kentucky

Copyright © 2014 by Carol Goodman Heizer, M.Ed. All rights reserved. Published by Alpha Consulting, a division of Alpha Consulting. 2014, with permission of the author.

Except for brief quotations and excerpts as permitted under the United States Copyright Act of 1976, no part of the publication may be reproduced or distributed in any form or means, whether in print or electronic, without written permission of the author or publisher.

ISBN-10: 1929251025
ISBN-13: **978-1-929251-02-5**
Additional copies available on-line at
createspace.com/4744753

Proudly printed and bound in the United States of America.

Cover photos by Carol Goodman Heizer
Copyright © 2014 by Carol Goodman Heizer
All rights reserved
Cover design by:
Carol Goodman Heizer and Mary Dow Smith

Dedicated -

*To all women
In all seasons of life.
To those in Spring –
May you be blessed by your youth.
To those in Summer –
May you be blessed by your busy life.
To those in Fall –
May you be blessed by your Golden Years.
To those in Winter –
May you be blessed by your legacy.*

Table of Contents

Introduction . . . iii

Chapter 1: SPRING
- Introduction . . 1
- All Things New . 3
- Exploring the World . 5
- Bright Colors . . 7
- Youth . . . 9
- Fearless . . 11
- Impatient . . 13
- Beginning To Bloom . 15
- Beauty . . 17
- Self-Discovery . 19

Chapter 2: SUMMER
- Introduction . . 23
- Activity . . 27
- Family . . 29
- Home . . 31
- Job . . . 35
- Friends . . 37
- Rushing . . 39
- Hobbies . . 41
- Cautious . . 43
- Empty Nest . . 45

Chapter 3: FALL
- Introduction . . 49
- Golden Years . . 51
- Retirement . . 53
- Friends . . 55
- Hobbies . . 57
- Value of Youth . 59

Compassion	61
Wisdom	63
Contemplation	65

Chapter 4: WINTER

Introduction	67
Declining Years	69
Gray Hair	71
Illness	73
Scars	75
Reflecting on Life	77
Future Generations	79
Legacy	81
Death	83

About the Author	*85*

INTRODUCTION

As with all forms of life – animal and plant – women, too, pass through their seasons of life.

In Spring, we burst forth with life, blooming into our "girl-womanhood" as we enjoy the earlier days of our lives, often characterized by the fearlessness and impatience that accompanies youth.

In Summer, we find ourselves busy with the demands of hearth and heart, as we enjoy the middle days of our lives, often characterized by rushing—yet cautious.

In Fall, we enjoy the status of Senior Citizens as we enjoy our greater freedom in the latter days of our lives, often characterized by our appreciation for youth—yet grateful for the wisdom we have gained.

In Winter, we enjoy reflecting back on our seasons and our heritage, as we prepare for our final days, often characterized by illness—yet focusing on future generations and our legacy to the world around us and especially to those we love.

Chapter 1
SPRING

Just as Spring bursts forth in the early months of the year, so it is with the young "girl-woman." She is fascinated with all the first-hand experiences to which she is exposed as she develops her five senses. She begins investigating her world and is intrigued by the variety of brilliant hues that surround her.

She is bursting forth in her energetic adolescence and feels so alive. She has not learned the value of fear and feels she can do anything her young heart desires. Her greatest frustration is her impatience with those around her and the world in general. Her world is so full of excitement and wonder that she wants to do it *all* and do it *now*!

As the flowers burst forth with life in Spring and give the world their gifts of color and fragrance, she, too, is bursting forth with new life—in body, mind, and spirit, It is a wondrous time, yet strange and frightening at times.

She becomes aware of her outer self and the young womanly beauty that is quickly unfolding. With the outer image she presents to the world, she finds herself examining every aspect of it—her skin, her eyes, her hair, her clothing. She feels the same in some small ways, yet vastly different in others, and this conflicting state of being causes her great confusion on many occasions.

She becomes more familiar with her external features and allows herself to travel the road leading to the next phase of her springtime journey. She begins looking inward and is sometimes surprised at what she finds. The earlier days of her life that brought pleasure and fun now bore her. They were things of her childhood and appropriate for only a child. Those days are now in her past, and they should be placed in her own personal history book of life.

As she steps into the days of womanhood and all of its expectations and responsibilities, she wonders how well she will do. Life up until this point ahs been rather comfortable and secure—surrounded with the protection of her family and loved ones.

Spring is past, and Summer is beginning to appear on the horizon. But now—what lies ahead?

Does she sometimes wish she could retreat into her earlier days of comfort and fun?

Will she have the inner resources to meet the challenges that lie ahead?

Some might label her as an apprentice at life, not knowing her trade but ready and willing to learn.

All Things New

There's a world out there I'm starting to see
With all kinds of things I've never known.
Some of the things, I know their names -
But other things, I haven't a clue.

I want to touch them, smell them, and taste
To see if I like them or send them away.
I'll take my time – not decide in haste
So I don't live to regret my foolish choice.

So many things, they're all so new
Whoever thought of these things to make?
They certainly had a mind so sharp
To conceive of these things, these all things new.

Exploring the World

My world is growing and getting larger
And in my excitement, I want to go -
Go to the East and go to the West,
Go to the North and go to the South.

I want to see everything that's way out there -
To hear the thunder and see the stars,
To meet the people and eat their food,
To swim in the ocean and fly in the sky.

To touch the ice on the snow-capped mount,
To put my foot in the icy stream,
To romp in the valley far below,
And smell the flowers that grow by the fence.

I'm part of this world – it's partly mine,
So I lay my claim to my special spot.
I'm ready to go, my bags are packed,
I want to get moving in exploring the world.

Bright Colors

So many colors this world has for me –
Some are dark and not so inviting,
But the other colors are the ones I like –
The blues, the reds, the greens, the yellows.

They remind me of Spring and my life today
As I find my spirit is drawn to them now.
They represent life and fun and joy,
So I take my colors – only the bright.

I'll leave the others for other girls
Who may be quiet or slow to explore.
Those who may like the darker shades –
But for me, I choose only bright colors.

Youth

I hear them say when they often talk
That energy is wasted on lively youth.
But I don't feel my energy is wasted –
How else would I live my fullest life?

I still play games and have my fun,
I like my friends and french fries, too.
Sometimes I think I even like school,
And soccer games when bigger boys play.

I feel like I'm strong and very brave, too;
I'm not afraid of thunder and lightning.
But I don't like snakes and big black spiders,
So I'm proud of my strength and bravery, too.

I'm no longer just a little girl,
I'm learning my way in this big old world.
I'm growing older and smarter, too.
I'm proud of myself, especially my youth.

Fearless

They tell me, "Be careful," and "Don't do that."
They're always warning, "Don't take chances."
I wonder why they're so very afraid.
I know what I'm doing. I always do.

But they keep warning and being concerned,
You'd think I don't have a brain in my head.
I tell them always, "You shouldn't worry,
I know what I'm doing. I always do."

I rode my bike in the street one day -
The way they acted you'd think I had died.
They're always fussing and scolding me.
I tell them "I know, I know, I know."

Older people seem so afraid,
Always saying what NOT to do.
They don't understand - I take care of myself,
I'm not afraid - I'm a fearless girl.

Impatient

They want me to slow down and take my time.
I tell them I try – I just can't seem to wait.
There's so much to see and do and feel,
I want to get on with my life right now.

They're always saying, "You have plenty of time,
Enjoy your life, take each day as it comes."
I know I should, but I'm in such a hurry
To do all I want and everything else.

I feel like I'm chained and made to go slow.
My spirit says, "Move. Get out of my way!"
They just do not know my lively spirit,
Or they'd let me go at my very own pace.

I don't want to grow old and move so slow
As the ones around me always do.
I like my life and the speed I go
Even if I am a little impatient.

Beginning To Bloom

My body is changing –
It's changing shape.
I'm no longer a stick
Straight up and down.

I'm developing breasts,
My hips are more rounded,
My legs now have calves,
And my nails are shaped.

My insides, too, are changing now.
My feelings are intense nearly every day.
They say it's my hormones, I don't know.
I just know I'm feeling strange.

I look in the mirror – I know it's me,
But at times I feel like I'm someone else.
Today was the day – I'm a "woman" now –
Not sure if I like it – this "monthly thing."

It's just part of my new life, they're telling me –
I'll adjust to the routine as months go by.
I'm trusting they're right – I hope they are.
I'm in a whole new world in this Spring of my life.

I'm like a flower in the Springtime fresh,
So bursting with life and energy, too.
But I have to wait – my time will come.
Yes, oh yes, I'm beginning to bloom.

Beauty

Each day in the mirror I see myself –
The freckles are fading, oh, at last.
My nails are filed and nicely polished.
I like the face I see in the mirror.

I'm wearing eye shadow and liner, too,
And even a smudge of pale pink blush.
My style in clothing has changed a lot,
And I wear my hair in different cuts.

I'm noticing boys, and they're noticing me.
Is it my looks or the clothes I wear?
Is it my smile or pretty eyes?
What do they think when they look at me?

All these things are only skin deep,
That's what I'm hearing from Mom and my aunts.
When I see them, I'm beginning to think
The beauty inside me is true, lasting beauty.

Self-Discovery

I'm in my twenties, I've grown quite a bit.
My body has changed, and so has my mind.
I'm starting to remember the words of others
And starting to see they were truly right.

My childish thoughts I've stored away
To keep as memories of days gone by.
I remember the thrill of finding new things
And thinking of exploring my big, wide world.

I remember my love of all those bright colors
And thinking somehow they made me "me."
The foolishness of children, though real to them,
Was cast aside for my youthful years.

Yes, I remember how fearless I was –
Nearly drove my parents to early graves.
They truly knew how foolish I was
As I crazily thought myself simply fearless.

And then the impatience that drove them wild
As they tried to explain there was always tomorrow.
But I couldn't listen, I wanted to "live" –
Live each day at break-neck speed.

Then there was the time I started to bloom –
Not just my body, but my inside too.
It was a cycle of fun and fear.
I knew who I was, but I wasn't sure.

Oh, the time I thought beauty was all.
I spent hours on my "outsides" trying to please.
Please WHO I'm not sure – was it THEM or ME?
But then I learned of true inner beauty.

I've made a discovery, most priceless of all.
I've discovered myself – perhaps not all.
At least it's a start, and I'm willing to bet
There's more to be found in the years ahead.

It's a journey I long for, knowing full well
It will hold bends and curves and dips.
But I've finally discovered the part of me
That holds real value because I'm ME.

Chapter 2
SUMMER

She sees the more carefree days of Spring as a memory to be treasured, for she now sees herself caught up in the daily routine and responsibilities of the Summer of her life. Her earlier days often dragged by as she wished to "grow up" and be on her own. But in looking back, she realizes the months and years sped by.

Her days are now filled with so many chores and tasks caring for her family and their endless needs and wants. She loves them deeply and wants to help, but she looks to the day when they can help themselves – and perhaps her, too.

Then there's the home she keeps up daily – the dusting and mopping and washing and ironing and cooking and dishes. She loves her home and wants it to speak well of her. As guests come to visit for the very first time, they see her influence in nearly every room. Her creativity is displayed throughout, and she simply desires to spend more time within its walls.

Her job takes her away the best hours of the day – when daylight has dawned and her energy is high. Then she remembers those women whose work hours are reversed. They work at night while others sleep, and sleep during the day when others work. She suddenly feels grateful for her own timetable and feels concern for the others whose internal clocks must run in reverse.

She values her friends and the time they spend together. Sometimes DOING – sometimes just BEING. However, she feels she sandwiches them in among her other assignments and regrets she hasn't more time for them, for they are often her lifeline to a renewed sense of energy and outside interests.

In taking an inventory of her life in general, she feels an overall sense of havoc – running here, running there, doing this, doing that. No time to stop – must keep going.

Being true to herself and the need for sanity, she does occasionally take time for special pastimes. Others may say she could use her time more wisely, but she knows there is a part of her that her hobbies keep alive. So, she will continue, knowing her time is well-spent, if for no one else other than herself.

She realizes now she has developed a sense of watchfulness that she disregarded in her

Spring. She is more prudent, particularly in reducing risk or danger, both to herself and others around her. She knows this comes with age, but she does wish she had developed it earlier in her youth. It may have saved her from some of the hurts and pitfalls in which she suddenly found herself.

Well, they say: "No use in crying over spilt milk." The past is over, and she did learn from her errors. Perhaps that was the reason she experienced them – to keep her from making them later in life when the hurts were deeper and the costs were higher.

How often she had longed for more tranquil days when she could have time to sit and think – to make a "wish list." To daydream. To quiet her mind. To merely stare into space.

Those days have arrived and, oh what a surprise! Perhaps "shock" would be a better word. They are not at all what she had envisioned. They are not the "dream come true." Quite the contrary.

Activity

The Spring of my life has slipped away –
It went by quickly, I hardly noticed
Until one day I suddenly saw
My youthful days were a thing of the past.

My life is full – so very full,
Sometimes I wonder where the hours go.
The clock keeps ticking as minutes fly.
I wish it would stop to give me more time.

I love my life, I wouldn't trade it.
I just need energy to keep me going.
I used to have that energy galore.
I wish I'd saved some for these busy times.

I'm happy in life, my lot is good.
I have the health to hurry about
Keeping appointment and luncheon dates
And, of course, the workouts at the local gym.

Family

My family is precious – every member.
No two are alike – yet much the same.
We share our lives, our likes, our dreams,
Yet live individually in our own special sphere.

We have our differences as all families do.
We even argue and fight now and then,
Each wanting to prove his or her own point,
Yet coming to gather in important matters.

Each of us comes from the family tree,
But we each branch out in our own direction –
Some going here, some going there,
Yet we all are bound to the same tree trunk.

Our roots grow deep to weather the storms,
To keep us standing in the winds of life,
We may have our unique little ways,
But love bonds us together now and always.

Home

Home is where the heart is,
that is true,
And my heart is beating in
every room.
They speak of memories and
days gone by,
But also tomorrows and the
dreams they hold.

I decorate my home with the
things I love –
The picture over the mantle of
my favorite place,
The picture in the dining room of
my parents long gone,
The quilts on my beds my
grandmother made.

My grandfather's coal bucket
sits in the den.

We use it to keep magazines in
their place.
My great-grandfather was a
handy carpenter,
And I have the table he made
for his bride.

The china I use for special
occasions
Came down through the family
to Mother and me.
We remember using it at
Grandma's house
Along with the meals we
shared with them.
Even my basement has special
treasures –
Not much value to the money-
minded,
But priceless to me for the
memories held.

No money on earth could buy
most of them.

The hand-made cradle my
father carved
And the wedding dress my
mother made,
The ragged doll I had as a
child.
Yes, my home is a treasure-house
full of love.

Job

*My daily job takes so much of my time,
I feel I almost live there instead of my home.
But bills must be paid, and I must eat,
So I go off to work and do my job.*

*It's really not bad, though I often complain.
It could be worse in so many ways.
I arrive before eight and leave at five,
With an hour for lunch it's not so tough.*

*I do my best on every task
To be proud of my work when I am done.
I always want the others to know
They can depend on me each and every day.*

*I'm helping my family and myself, too,
By earning honest wages
For an honest day's work.
I'll not complain and be grateful now.*

*With many off work and little to eat,
I will give thanks that I have a job
And count my blessings –
So many there are.*

Friends

My friends are many and varied, too –
Some like the movies, some like to sew,
Some like the Spring, some like the Fall.
But we all have the bond of womanhood.

We get together as time permits
Though not as often as we would like.
Our jobs and families – they take
our time,
So we often have to cancel our plans.

We talk of hobbies and things we enjoy,
Though our talk often turns to desires
and dreams.
We take our time to gather as friends
To escape the duties and chores of
our days.

We laugh and giggle and tell funny tales,
Each one out-doing the other with smiles.
But our time together soon comes
to a close
As we bid farewell till we meet again.

Rushing

My day is so busy, I never have time
To do all the things I need to do.
From dawn till dusk I never stop
And fall into bed with weary bones.

I plan each day to allow some time,
Yet never it seems that time unfolds.
Something new comes along –
that time is gone,
And another day over with no free time.

I feel like a mouse on that
spinning wheel,
Always running but getting nowhere.
Never stopping to catch my breath,
Always tired and no time to rest.

Perhaps some day the time will come
When life quiets down and I can
slow down.
But for now I'll daily give my thanks
For life and health to keep up the pace.

Rushing

Now that I am older I have time
to do things I need to do
and days seem to never stop
and nights to be lovely, having time

...

Hobbies

Some say hobbies are a waste of time
With nothing to show but my creative self.
"What a waste of time these hobbies take;
Time better spent," they often say.

Hobbies truly are a valued retreat –
An escape from the world with its daily stress.
A time alone with just myself
To know ME better and use my skill.

Whether it be painting or crafting or writing a book,
I'll use my talent as best I can.
To enjoy my hobby and results it brings
And share with the world for all to enjoy.

But if not for the world and all to see,
Perhaps just for me and my own sense of pride –
To stand back and look at what I achieved
And say to myself, "A job well done."

Cautious

As I grow older I'm finding a new trend -
Where I once was fearless, now I am cautious.
Thinking of safety for myself and friends,
Especially family and those I love.

Where once I charged in like a raging bull,
Now I think twice before going forward.
I check my surroundings and look for danger,
And when all is safe, I go ahead.

I'm not clothed in fear – just a cautious nature
To ensure as much safety as I possibly can.
Perhaps it comes from my responsible self –
To know I am living the best I can.

The summer winds down, activities slow.
My body's still young, but I notice a change.
My mind is still sharp, and so is my wit,
But things around me are changing fast.

I look to the future and the days ahead,
And I see a quietness beginning to come.
I've never had this sense before –
It causes a disturbance within my soul.

Empty Nest

Now I know what the quietness meant
And the disturbance it caused
within my soul.
The children are gone – away from
my home,
The quiet is deafening and I want it gone.

I remember the days I wanted noise gone
And dreamed of the day when all
was neat.
I'd have time to myself to go or stay,
To be anything else or just be ME.

So often I remember their
ceaseless chatter
And wanted them just to hush for a spell.
I wanted them older to fend for
themselves,
To be more self-sufficient and give
me a break.

I remember the sports and the
many games
I often attended when bone-weary tired.
I remember the gymnastics and
ballet classes

I often sat through when other
chores called.

I remember those hurried and busy days
When all I wanted was to rest a bit.
But I made my way to games and classes
And wished for the day they'd all be done.

Now I long for the days of noise and
clutter –
The days the kids fought and wanted
their way,
The clutter of toys, the mess of rooms.
What I would give to have it all again.

Those days are gone, they cannot
come back
However I wish and hope and dream.
So I will keep those days so near –
Alive in my memory as long as I can.

Chapter 3
FALL

She bids farewell to the warmth of Summer and finds real joy in the colors of Fall. the reds, the golds, the oranges, the yellows – each brings joy to her color-loving spirit. She sits by the trees or walks in the woods – anything to soak in the beauty that surrounds her soul.

Yet as she enjoys the golden hues, she is all-too-aware that she, too, has stepped into her "golden years." Her greatest delight is leaving her job, for now she has time to enjoy herself – to do the things that bring her delight and satisfaction.

She wants time with her friends and be part of their lives – something she had little time for in the Summer of her life. She also looks forward to time of her own – to enjoy her favorite pastimes. She has sensed her creative energies building inside and longs to release them – to give them life.

In the midst of her anticipation of fun times to come, she also knows there's another aspect of Fall. As the days grow shorter and the nights grow longer, she has come to realize how far she has traveled in life, the lessons she has learned, and her concern of what the future holds.

She recognizes the difference between sympathy and compassion, the difference between knowledge and wisdom

She contemplates many things now – some happy memories and some sorrowful times. She knows that both she and all her sister-women have experienced both. She trusts that all of them are better citizens for what they have experienced.

She remembers the joy she felt at the beginning of Fall, along with her sense of sadness as it leads into the following season. She knows more changes will come and believes she will face them with all the grace and strength she has been given.

Golden Years

My life is different now – so
different, indeed.
I have come through the "empty nest,"
Though its effects often prick my soul.
Now I must move forward and look ahead.

They often call it "The Golden Years,"
This period of time I am now experiencing.
But when I think of gold, I know
Its value always lingers long.

So now I look at my life as gold
And wonder how I'll spend it.
I know my days are fewer now
Than in decades past when time rolled by.

I long for the energy I used to have
And be able to run the steps I did.
I now have stiffness in many joints
And my legs don't move as they often did.

My hands now have those ugly brown spots
I once abhorred on my grandmother's hands.
I used to tell her "Just walk straight,"
But now I know that's an impossible task.

Yet in spite of it all, I'm awfully glad
I am still around to enjoy my lot.
I'll take the aches and pains and all
To be here to enjoy another day.

I'll enjoy these days in the Fall of my life
And experience whatever that life hands me.
I often longed for my Golden Years –
But I had not counted the cost to me.

Retirement

It has finally come at the end of my work –
The time to relax and do as I want.
No alarm clock to go off in the morn
And no set time when the sun goes down.

I can sleep till noon or rise with the chickens,
I can eat breakfast first or maybe lunch.
I can listen to music or sew till dawn.
I can walk all day or write some poems.

My time is my own – it's finally here
To enjoy my days as I jolly well please.
No need to hurry – no need to rush,
But what a surprise I have found of late.

My days are as busy as they always were,
But now for things I always enjoy –
Time for the gym and aerobic classes,
Time to walk and chat with friends.

Time for my children, as friends we are –
Dealing with them as full-grown adults.
We talk together of many things –
They of their trials and me of mine.

This time of my life I fully enjoy
When time is a number on the old clicking clock.
I'll spend it my way to fully enjoy –
I earned it from work those many years.

Friends

My earlier friends, we ran and shopped
Always going, always active –
Never stopping to smell the roses,
Never stopping to watch the brook.

But now my friends and I have changed,
We're often content and just sit and talk –
To share the stories of our new-found freedom
Or sometimes complain of aches and pains.

The younger ones see us often as "old,"
But we know better – we're merely "seasoned."
I'm sure they look at our wrinkles and limps,
But we consider them as our battle scars.

My friends and I, we often discuss
How the young never see them-
selves as old.
But we know – we know as time passes
They, too, will see their bodies grow old.

So my friends enjoy our time.
We frequently say we are
"Comrades in arms."
We've walked the road that brought
us here
And continue to travel as long as we can.

Hobbies

For my many hobbies I now have time,
Not always rushed as in earlier days.
I can do it today, tomorrow, next week.
Time is my friend, I enjoy her more.

I used to think genealogy a bore,
And then I found my ancestral tree.
I suddenly found it a puzzle like,
Attempting to fit the pieces together.

The more I learned, the more I desired,
The more faces I found, I wanted others –
I wanted their stories – details and all,
I couldn't stop till I found it all.

But deep inside my mind I knew
I'd never know all, for some were lost.
I'd have to live with the missing branches
Of my very own ancestral tree.

Then I decided to begin scrapbooks –
Not the ones of old with gross brown paper.
I'd begin with new – the styles of today
With color pictures and acid-free
stickers.

And what a surprise I found one day
As I could do both in one grand hobby.
I'd gather the info and pictures of old
And highlight them in color and
odd-cut paper.

The end result was a glorious book,
Full of history from way far back,
But also recent for all to enjoy
So they, also, could discover
their family roots.

Value of Youth

I'm enjoying these years in the Fall
of my life,
But I also look back on my early Spring
When energy was boundless, each
day a surprise,
When my wit was quick and my steps
were swift.

I sometimes long for those days
to return
When my skin was tight and my walk
was light,
When movement came easy – no
thought before,
When I rose with a leap and hated
bedtime.

I took it or granted and thought it
would last.
I'd never grow old, I told myself –

I'd always stay young, I'd see to that –
The value of youth is its optimistic view.

The dreams always rising – the
wishes all new,
The hope that tomorrow will be
better by far.
The value of youth in the Spring of
my life,
The mountains I'd climb – the seas I
would sail.

Compassion

The rough spots in life have taught me
compassion
To show charity and grace to all
those In need,
To be merciful and kind to those who
have fallen,
To lend an ear to the hurting heart.

To be patient and forbearing to
slow of mind,
To always be flexible in demands
of others.
To mourn with others in times of sorrow
And be happy with them in their
joyful times.

To lend a hand when others are weak,
To give my money when others have none,
To give of myself till it sometimes hurts –
That's the compassion I've learned in the Fall.

Wisdom

I thought I was smart when I
was young –
Gave all the answers to impress
other folks.
I thought they'd admire me - I
didn't know
They spoke of me joking and
called me a fool.

Then Spring passed to Summer
– I knew much more,
Still hadn't a clue how much to
be learned.
But the hard times came, and I
learned even more,
I had a grasp on that thing
called "knowledge."

But I hadn't learned at that
point in my life
The enormous difference between
knowledge and wisdom.
The years passed by and Summer
became Fall,
And with it came my big revelation.

I realized then that knowledge was facts —
Accumulating facts and nothing more.
But wisdom, I saw, was discernment,
sound judgment.
It'd taken me years to learn that truth.

I became insightful and perceptive, too -
Aware of my world — it's relation to me.
But most important, I finally learned
To be truly wise, you advance in your years.

Contemplation

As leaves start to fall and the sun grows cool,
The shadows lengthen and the air becomes chilled.
I find myself indoors more often
Especially in evening as it grows still darker.

It was always here then – but not always now.
Its warmth seems precious as it begins to fade,
The nights grow longer and often cold.

My bones feel the change and so do my joints.
The critters all scurry to store in their food
While finding homes for long winter naps.
The Fall is ending, 'twill soon be gone.

Chapter 4
WINTER

She sees the trees' bare limbs and the leaves on the ground, along with spindly stalks that once held flowers. Fall has slipped into the history books of time, and Winter is upon her. But just as the white hair covers her head, so does the snow cover the earth. Yet beneath both, she knows, still lives life – just resting a bit.

She sees her life, framed by her declining years, and knows that sickness and scars of life will be readily seen by herself and others. She also knows, as she looks back on her life, she trusts she made a difference in the lives of those around her in particular and to the world in general.

She has lived a good life although it had its darker moments; she also knows that life held both mountain-top and lower-valley for all who traveled life's road. She has also learned that she could not see around the bends, but she would find the strength to handle whatever would lie beyond that curve.

She thinks of her descendants yet to come, along with those who already make up her family tree. She does this not with a sense of dismay or alarm but with a sense of gratitude for a life well-lived and a sense of appreciation for all the blessings that have been bestowed upon her.

She faces her final days with an awareness and acceptance that death is a part of her life cycle. She has lived a good life.

> She has lived a long life.
> And she is grateful.

Declining Years

The final rays of the Fall sun have faded,
Slipped beneath the horizon to be seen
no more.
The cold of Winter has descended now,
And the chill in the air brings many thoughts.

I realize it now – my advancing years
And as they advance, my health declines.
I knew it would come – I truly did,
But I pushed it aside to the back of my mind.

I didn't want to think of these days
And the trials that were certain to come.
I tried my best to DO my best,
But it wasn't enough to stave off the Winter.

Now it has come, and I must accept –
Accept with grace and courage, also
The days ahead will be hard at best,
Yet I'll continue on 'til I can't go on.

Gray Hair

There's life under the blanket of my
own gray hair,
So don't sell me short and think I am gone.
My mind is sharp, my wit in tact
Though I may sometimes forget a word.

That blanket of hair is a covering for me.
It speaks of my life and the wisdom I've gained.
My skin is wrinkled, but it tells a tale
Of facing life with a strong, robust will.

The gray on my head doesn't mean
I am dead –
I'm far from that – I'm living still.
But I know as the clock continues to tick,
The symptoms set in and I'll start to fail.

Be kind to me and show me respect.
The gray hair I'm carrying is my badge of life.
I once was young and awkward, too,
But now I carry myself with grace
and poise.

Illness

I tried, I tried, I really tried
To keep myself healthy and free of germs.
But try as I might, I couldn't stay well.
I'm frequently bothered with sickness
and pain.

I try to be brave and not complain,
But the weight of affliction takes it toll.
The ill health comes, I cannot escape,
So I cope with the pain and take my meds.

I never imagined in my Springtime days
That illness could consume both body
and mind.
I fear I will fail in my battle with this
And not be the victor in the struggle
for life.

Please help me, God– please help me, Lord
To conquer my fear of what lies ahead.
I'll not give in, I'll not give up.
I'll face the challenge, I'll attempt the feat.

Scars

I often look at the scars on my skin
And remember the time they first appeared.
I can remember the day and often the hour.
I certainly recall the official cause.

Some have faded and are nearly gone,
While others remain in original form.
The pain they caused has long gone away,
So I'm not concerned that they live on my skin.

The scars that are deepest and cause greatest pain
Are the ones that are found on my heart and soul.
The scar of losing a long-sought goal,
The scar of rejection, the scar of hate.

The scar of losing a loved one young,
Too early in life they went to the grave.
The scar of living each lonely day
Without hearing their voice or seeing their smile.

These are the scars that are deep within
That no one sees, yet I bear their pain -
The pain that lasts and doesn't depart,
But I'll carry on in spite of the scars.

Reflecting on Life

I have time now that I can't get around
To think on my life over years and years.
I go back in my mind to my
Springtime days
And fun of my youth with beauty
and color.

As I discovered my world, I discovered myself,
And that was a mighty scary trip.
Then came Summer and my busy life.
I hadn't a minute to think of myself.

I learned to be cautious and think
things through.
As the years wore on, and I got
some "smarts."
Too bad I had waited so many years
To gain such wisdom I needed in youth.

But that season, too, eventually ended
And I found myself in the Fall of life.
It brought its own problems, but
good things, too.
Then I entered this season, this Winter season.

I'm still going on, I know not its end.
I can say with glad heart
I lived and endured my trials with grit.
This Winter I'm chilled in body and spirit.

I've lived through the "year" –
four seasons in all.
They all have been different in many ways,
Each with its blessings, trials, and hurts,
But I've managed to survive them
one at a time.

Future Generations

As I look back over the years through
my life,
I see the lessons I learned through
hard work,
Along with lessons from family and friends.
They came through the time we
spent together.

We had few gadgets – no electronic stuff.
In my earlier years, we called them
DOODADS.
We made our own fun – indoors and out.
We used our energy and our minds as well.

We made our own toys and fanciful tricks –
It did our brains good to think up such things.
But kids today – I worry 'bout them.
They go to the store and buy all they want.

They'll never know the fun of "home-made"
And never the fun of "building" with friends.
They're out by themselves with store-bought things,
Never feeling the glee of "I made it myself."

Another thing troubles me 'bout today's
young folks –
In my years gone by with strong family ties,
The family bond was strong as oak,
But today's family trees, I see falling apart.

But, perhaps, in the days yet to come
The good old traditions will
return once more
When families grow strong and
the ties remain
To make the world better – yes,
better by far.

Legacy

As I near the end of my days on earth,
I think of my will and the things I will leave
To those who loved me and knew me well.
I'm thinking not of material things.

My possessions are special – I've held them dear,
But they are things that can be bought and sold.
So they're not my priority in Winter months
As many might think as I near the end.

<u>To Them I Bequeath:</u>
My love of nature as God did provide,
My love for animals He created also –
To care for them both and keep them alive
For others to see and tend and hold.

My joy in the Springtime of years gone by
When life burst forth in so many forms.
My love of Summer when family and friends
Gave such a dimension to my life back then.

My pleasure at seeing Fall come around
With its colors and beauty of its very own kind.
To see the various forms of life
Preparing to rest in the long days ahead.

My thoughts and my prayers as
Winter came in
To know that beneath the blanket of snow
Lie forms of life ready to burst forth
In the soon-coming days of
Springtime again.

Death

Many fear death and quake at its prospect,
But I am not one – not one of those,
For I know that death is part of living –
That death awaited since the day I was born.

I feared it, of course, in my earlier years,
Not wanting it to come to those I held dear,
Not wanting it to come to me because
I had much to do and wanted to live.

But as Fall wore on and I lived my life,
And those I knew began to die,
I realized they lived in my spirit and heart –
Though body was gone, their life lived on.

As my older friends grew so sick and weak,
They longed for their "friend" – some called it death,
For in their hearts they truly knew
Life doesn't end at the graveyard plot.

They felt in their hearts, believed in their minds
That what awaited them on the other side
Was far better than life on this old earth,
So they looked to the day as they crossed over

That a life well-spent
Is a life well-lived.

Carol Goodman Heizer, M.Ed. is an eight-time published author, speaker, and professional training and development leader whose books have sold both in the United States and overseas.

She holds a Bachelor of Arts degree in Drama and Public Speaking from Asbury College in Wilmore, Kentucky, and an M.Ed. in Secondary Education with concentration in English and Literature from the University of Louisville (Kentucky).

After teaching middle school and high school English and Writing for 17 years, Carol opened Alpha Consulting and began speaking to various business, industrial, and educational groups. In addition, she conducted professional training and development seminars for clients such as the Department of Defense, Holiday Inn of America, Humana, the Louisville Board of Realtors, the Courier-Journal, General Electric, Purdue University, and Underwriters Safety and Claims.

Recognizing the need for her own personal and professional growth, Carol has been a Kentucky Speakers Association board member, and an active member of the National Speakers Association, Louisville Area Chamber of Commerce, Louisville/Jefferson County Convention and

Visitor's Bureau, Kentuckiana Chapter of the American Society for Training and Development, Kentucky Society of Association Executives, and Ohio Christian Schools organization. She is also a member of Louisville Christian Writers and Kentucky Christian Writers.

Carol was a columnist for several years for *Today's Woman* magazine, *International Clowning* newsletter, and the Louisville, Kentucky, chapter of *Friendship Force International* newsletter. She also designed and wrote the quarterly newsletter for the Louisville Metro (Kentucky) Revenue Commission while employed there.

She has hosted the local CNN affiliate WNAI radio station's call-in program titled *I've Been Thinking* that addressed local issues and featured individuals within the community who had a positive influence on their world.

Her stories have appeared in several editions of *Chicken Soup for the Soul*. She has also had various articles appear in *Christian Communicator*, a professional publication of American Christian Writers.

Once asked how she ever kept up with her busy schedule, she replied, "I believe my life is a self-promoting cycle. "What I am accomplishing brings me so much pleasure that it continues to give me more energy."

www.ingramcontent.com/pod-product-compliance
Lightning Source LLC
Chambersburg PA
CBHW071311040426
42444CB00009B/1969